FIRST 50 SONGS

YOU SHOULD PLAY ON AUTOHARP

Arranged by Fred Sokolow

Editorial assistance by Ronny S. Schiff

ISBN 978-1-5400-8346-3

Hal•Leonard®

Visit Hal Leonard Online at
www.halleonard.com

Contact us:
Hal Leonard
7777 West Bluemound Road
Milwaukee, WI 53213
Email: info@halleonard.com

In Europe, contact:
Hal Leonard Europe Limited
42 Wigmore Street
Marylebone, London, W1U 2RN
Email: info@halleonardeurope.com

In Australia, contact:
Hal Leonard Australia Pty. Ltd.
4 Lentara Court
Cheltenham, Victoria, 3192 Australia
Email: info@halleonard.com.au

CONTENTS

About the Author

Fred Sokolow is best known as the author of over a hundred and fifty instructional and transcription books and DVDs for guitar, banjo, Dobro, mandolin, lap steel and ukulele. Fred has long been a well-known West Coast multi-string performer and recording artist, particularly on the acoustic music scene. The diverse musical genres covered in his books and DVDs, along with several bluegrass, jazz and rock recordings he has released, demonstrate his mastery of many musical styles. Whether he's playing Delta bottleneck blues, bluegrass or old-time banjo, '30s swing guitar or screaming rock solos, he does it with authenticity and passion. You can see him play autoharp on YouTube at https://www.youtube.com/watch?v=4IXtiziBJlk

Email Fred with any questions about this or his other books at sokolowmusic.com

Introduction

Ever since Maybelle Carter showed the world that you could do more than strum an autoharp—you could actually *fingerpick* melodies—the players have gotten better and better and the instrument has achieved more popularity. There are several annual autoharp gatherings around the U.S., there's an autoharp Hall of Fame, an excellent magazine devoted to the instrument, and a growing number of virtuoso players and teachers. If you search on YouTube, you'll find countless videos of people playing music of many genres on the instrument, and audio from many recently released solo autoharp albums.

This book is a collection of songs arranged in keys that are autoharp-friendly, with strumming-pattern suggestions. The tunes represent many genres: folk, country, pop, bluegrass, old-time and more. Many of the songs have been performed and recorded by Hall-of-Fame autoharp players like Bryan Bowers, Maybelle Carter, Kilby Snow, Mike Seeger, Will Smith and Karen Mueller.

Due to its growing popularity, the autoharp itself has been evolving and improving. The old Oscar Schmidt models typically had fifteen chords; most modern autoharps have twentyone, which makes it possible to play songs with more complex chord progressions, and to play songs in more than a few keys. Boutique luthiers are building autoharps made of fine woods and beautiful design. There are also diatonic autoharps, which are made to be played in just one key. They have fewer chords but a fuller sound, as many of the notes are doubled up. Consequently, many virtuoso players carry a suitcase full of diatonic autoharps, each built for a particular key.

If you already play autoharp, this song list is certain to expand your repertoire. If you don't, this will get you started!

Enjoy!

Fred Sokolow

PS: A strumming pattern is written at the beginning of each song. The up- and down-arrows tell you to strum down with your thumb or up with your fingers. The rhythm slashes under the arrows are quarter notes or eighth notes; they indicate timing. For example:

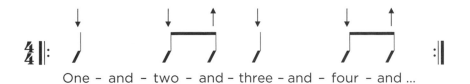

One – and – two – and – three – and – four – and ...

Amazing Grace

Words by John Newton
Traditional American Melody

John Newton, naval serviceman/slave trader*/poet/evangelical cleric, wrote the words to this famous hymn in 1772; the melody was added in 1835 when composer William Walker adapted the melody of a shape-note song, "New Britain," to Newton's lyrics. Various legends surrounding Newton have inspired several movies, and the song is perhaps the most popular English language hymn tune of all time. You'll find many autoharp renditions of the hymn on YouTube.

*Newton ran slave ships for Britain, but saw the error of his ways and became a fervent fighter for the abolition of slavery in England.

Additional Lyrics

3. When we've been there ten thousand years, bright shining as the sun;
   We'll have no less days to sing God's praise than when we first begun.

Greensleeves

Sixteenth Century Traditional English

This English ballad goes all the way back to the 1500s, and is also a popular Christmas song when sung with a different set of lyrics ("What Child Is This?"). Shakespeare mentioned the song in his *The Merry Wives of Windsor*. It was said to be John F. Kennedy's favorite song. U.K. autoharpist, Heather Farrell Roberts has a beautiful version on YouTube.

Additional Lyrics

2. Your vows you've broken, like my heart, oh, why did you so enrapture me?
   Now I remain in a world apart, but my heart remains in captivity.

3. I have been ready at your hand, to grant whatever you would crave.
   I have both wagered life and land, your love and good-will for to have.

Angels from Montgomery

Words and Music by John Prine

John Prine's "Angels from Montgomery" is probably his most-recorded song. He wrote it in 1971 as a sort of sequel to "Hello in There," another tune that comments on the dissatisfaction, loneliness and sadness of many elderly people. According to some sources, "Angels from Montgomery" is an expression, originating in Alabama, meaning a last-minute pardon for a prisoner from the governor. The song describes an old woman who feels imprisoned by her tedious, unsatisfying life.

Make me a post - er of an old ro - de - o. ___

Just give me one ___ thing ___ that I can hold on ___ to.

To be - lieve ___ in this liv - in' is just a ___ hard way to go. ___

1., 2.

C   G

3.

C   G

Additional Lyrics

2. When I was a young girl, I had me a cowboy.
   He weren't much to look at, just a free, ramblin' man.
   But that was a long time, and no matter how I try,
   The years just flow by like a broken-down dam.

3. There's flies in the kitchen, I can hear them a-buzzin',
   And I ain't done nothin' since I woke up today.
   How in the hell can a person go to work in the mornin',
   And come home in the evening and have nothing to say.

Blowin' in the Wind

Words and Music by Bob Dylan

When it was written in 1962, "Blowin' in the Wind" was a major breakthrough for Dylan and all his folksinging peers. Along with "A Hard Rain's A-Gonna Fall," it raised the bar, lyrically, for songwriters everywhere. A few months after it appeared on Dylan's second album (1963's *The Freewheelin' Bob Dylan*), Peter, Paul and Mary's version of the song became a huge pop hit. It has been recorded by hundreds of artists in many languages and is forever linked with protests, the civil rights movement and progressive causes. Dylan later acknowledged that the song is his adaptation of "No More Auction Block for Me," an old spiritual that was sung by former slaves.

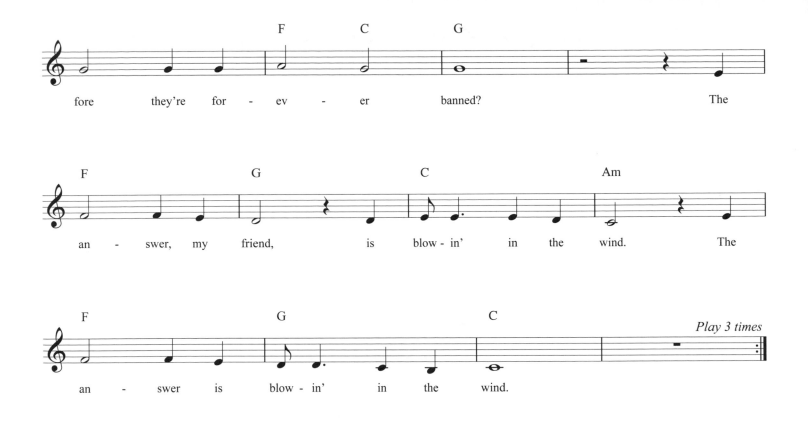

fore they're for - ev - er banned? The

an - swer, my friend, is blow - in' in the wind. The

Play 3 times

an - swer is blow - in' in the wind.

Additional Lyrics

2. How many years must a mountain exist, before it is washed to the sea?
How many years can some people exist, before they're allowed to be free?
How many times can a man turn his head, and pretend that he just doesn't see?
The answer, my friend, is blowin' in the wind. The answer is blowin' in the wind.

3. How many times must a man look up before he can see the sky?
How many ears must one man have before he can hear people cry?
How many deaths will it take 'til he knows that too many people have died?
The answer, my friend, is blowin' in the wind. The answer is blowin' in the wind.

Blue Eyes Crying in the Rain

Words and Music by Fred Rose

"Blue Eyes Crying in the Rain" was already thirty years old when Willie Nelson scored a #1 hit with it in 1975. (Roy Acuff recorded it in 1947, Hank Williams in 1951.) It was penned by the great songwriter/producer Fred Rose, who also wrote "No One Will Ever Know," "The End of the World," "Roly Poly" and many of Hank Williams' hits. "Blue Eyes..." appeared on the *Red-Headed Stranger* album, which propelled Willie Nelson to stardom.

1. In the twi - light glow I see _____ her blue eyes cry - in' in the rain. When we kissed good - bye _____ and part - ed, I knew we'd nev - er meet a - gain. Love _____ is like a dy - ing em - ber, on - ly mem - o - ries re - main. Through _____ the a - ges, I'll re - mem - ber blue eyes cry - in' in the rain.

2. Now my hair has turned to sil - ver. All my life I've loved in vain. I can see her star _____ in heav - en, blue eyes cry - in' in the rain. Some - day when we meet up yon - der, we'll stroll hand - in - hand a - gain, in _____ a land that knows no part - ing, blue eyes cry - in' in the rain.

Bury Me Beneath the Willow

Traditional

This is the first song the Carter Family recorded in 1927, at the famous Bristol Sessions where they and Jimmie Rodgers were discovered. The tune was archived by a music professor in 1906, and it probably is much older than that. The verse and chorus share the same melody.

Additional Lyrics

2. When they told me that he did not love me, I could not believe it was true,
   Until an angel softly whispered, "He has proven untrue to you."

3. Tomorrow was our wedding day, but oh, Lord, oh where is he?
   He's gone to seek him another bride and he cares no more for me.

4. Oh, bury me under the violets blue, to prove my love to him.
   Tell him that I would die to save him, for his love I never could win.

Crazy

Words and Music by Willie Nelson

In 1961, when Willie Nelson composed the jazzy torch song, "Crazy," he had already penned several country hits, but was relatively unknown as a performer. Many singers in the country, jazz and pop genres have recorded it, but Patsy Cline's 1961 version is a timeless classic—the Guinness Book of World Records said it was the song "most played on juke boxes all over the world." The song includes some diminished chords, which are lacking on most autoharps, but the arrangement that follows has some chords written in parentheses, which make good substitutes for the missing diminished chords. They can also be omitted to make the tune a bit easier to play.

Do You Believe in Magic

Words and Music by John Sebastian

John Sebastian wrote and recorded "Do You Believe in Magic" in 1964 for his pop/rock group,
The Lovin' Spoonful, and it became a Top Ten hit that year. It has been covered by many artists and has
been heard in the soundtracks to multiple movies and TV shows. Sebastian, whose roots are in folk music,
played an amplified autoharp in the recording, and he was certain the instrument had never before been
used on a pop record.

Additional Lyrics

2. Do you believe in magic? Don't bother to choose
   If it's jug band music or rhythm and blues,
   Just go and listen, and it'll start with a smile
   That won't wipe off your face no matter how hard you try.
   Your feet start tappin' and you can't seem to find
   How you got there, so just blow your mind!

3. If you believe in magic, come along with me.
   We'll dance until mornin' 'til there's just you and me,
   And maybe, if the music is right,
   I'll meet you tomorrow sorta late at night,
   And we'll go dancin', baby, then you'll see
   How the magic's in the music and the music's in me, yeah!
   Do you believe in magic? Yeah!
   Believe in the magic of a young girl's soul,
   Believe in the magic of rock and roll,
   Believe in the magic that can set you free.
   Aw! Talkin' 'bout the magic.

Fly Around, My Pretty Little Miss

Traditional

This old-timey folk song/fiddle tune was recorded by numerous string bands in the 1920s, including Frank Blevins and his Tar Heel Rattlers, the Skillet Lickers, and (with alternate titles) the Bogtrotters and the Hillbillies…and it continues to be recorded and performed by old-time string bands, bluegrassers and soloists today. Bill Monroe based his version of "Shady Grove" on this lively song, and you can see and hear contemporary autoharp virtuoso Karen Mueller perform it on her website. It's often played as an instrumental fiddle tune, but there are countless verses when it is performed with vocals. Like most fiddle tunes, it has two sections, an A part and a B part, each of which is played twice in a row. Once you've played AABB, you've gone once around the tune. I've never heard lyrics sung to the B part of "Fly Around."

Additional Lyrics

2. Peaches in the summertime, apples in the fall;
   If I can't have the one I love, I'll have no one at all.

3. Higher up the cherry tree, the sweeter grow the cherries.
   The more you hug and kiss the girls, the more they want to marry.

4. If you see my pretty little miss, if you see my darlin',
   If you see my pretty little miss, tell her I'm goin' to Harlan.

5. Coffee grows on white oak trees, the river flows with brandy;
   If I had that pretty little miss, I'd feed her sugar candy.

Freight Train

Words and Music by Elizabeth Cotten

Elizabeth "Libba" Cotten grew up in North Carolina and wrote "Freight Train" when she was a teenager, inspired by the trains roaring by on tracks near her home. Later in life, the Seeger family employed her as a housekeeper in Washington D.C. and discovered that she sang and fingerpicked the guitar "upside down" (she was left handed but did not re-string the guitar). Mike Seeger helped get her started performing, recording and touring on the folk and blues circuits, and she continued to do so well into her eighties. Budding fingerpickers used to be required to learn "Freight Train," and some of Cotten's other compositions have also become often-recorded folk favorites.

Verse

Brightly, in 2

1. Freight train, freight train, run so fast, _____
2. When I'm dead and in my grave, _____
3. *See additional lyrics*

freight train, freight train, run so fast, _____
no more good times run here I crave. _____

please don't tell what train I'm on, so they won't
Place the stones at my head and feet so and tell them

know what _____ route I have gone.
all that I'm gone to _____ sleep.

Play 3 times

Additional Lyrics

3. When I die, Lord, bury me deep, way down on old Chestnut Street,
   So I can hear old Number Nine as she comes rollin' by.

Goodnight, Irene

Words and Music by Huddie Ledbetter and John A. Lomax

Huddie Ledbetter, also known as Leadbelly, said he learned "Goodnight, Irene" from his uncles. His reworking of the song has made it a timeless, classic campfire song. In 1951, Pete Seeger's folk group, The Weavers, scored a #1 pop hit with their version of "Goodnight, Irene." Covers soon followed by Frank Sinatra and a great many pop and country artists. A convict who was pardoned by the governor of Texas because of his prowess as a singer and performer on 12-string guitar, Leadbelly also gave us "Midnight Special," "Cotton Fields," "Rock Island Line" and "Where Did You Sleep Last Night" (also called "In the Pines"). Leadbelly died in 1949 but his musical influence can't be overstated! A Leadbelly recording of "Cotton Fields" turned Bob Dylan on to folk music and set him on his incredible career path. Lonnie Donegan's covers of Leadbelly tunes started the skiffle music craze in England, which inspired the Beatles to begin playing music…and the hits keep coming: In 1994, Nirvana performed "Where Did You Sleep Last Night" in their *MTV Unplugged* concert/album. (Note: in the chorus of "Goodnight, Irene," Leadbelly sang "I get you in my dreams," but the Weavers' and most subsequent versions have "I'll see you in my dreams.")

Chorus

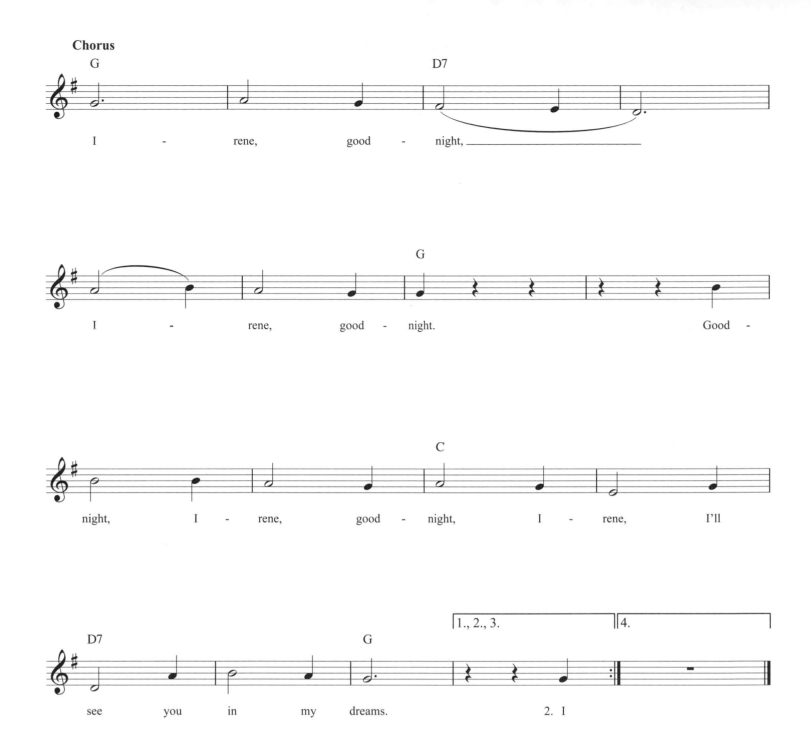

I - rene, good - night, _____ I - rene, good - night. Good -

night, I - rene, good - night, I - rene, I'll

see you in my dreams. 2. I

Additional Lyrics

2. I asked your mother for you, she told me that you were too young.
   I wish to the Lord I'd never seen your face; I'm sorry you ever was born.

3. Stop ramblin' and stop gamblin', quit stayin' out late at night.
   Go home to your wife and your family, sit down by the fireside bright.

4. I love Irene, God knows I do. I'll love her 'til the sea runs dry.
   But if Irene turns her back on me, I'm gonna take morphine and die.

Hallelujah

Words and Music by Leonard Cohen

Canadian singer/songwriter Leonard Cohen recorded "Hallelujah" in 1984. His record company refused to release it as a single, but it was included on his *Various Positions* LP. A few years later Bob Dylan began performing it in concerts. John Cale recorded it in 1991, and his version was included in the 2001 movie *Shrek*, garnering a huge audience for the song. Jeff Buckley's 1994 version received critical acclaim but did not become a hit until 2007, ten years after his untimely death. Rufus Wainwright's later cover further popularized "Hallelujah," and to date it has been recorded by over three hundred artists and has been included in the soundtracks of many movies and TV shows. (Cohen stated he wrote over 80 verses for the song initially, and there are many alternate verses penned by other performers.)

1. I've heard there was ___ a se-cret chord ___ that Da-vid played ___ and it
2.–5. *See additional lyrics*

pleased the Lord, ___ but you don't real-ly care for mu - sic,

do ya? ___ Well, it goes like this: the

fourth, the fifth, the mi - nor fall and the ma - jor lift, the

baf - fled king ___ com - pos - ing Hal - le - lu - jah. ___

Chorus

Hal - le - lu - jah,   Hal - le - lu - jah,

Hal - le - lu - jah,   Hal - le -

lu - jah.

2. Well, your

Additional Lyrics

2. Well, your faith was strong but you needed proof. You saw her bathing on the roof.
Her beauty and the moonlight overthrew ya.
She tied you to her kitchen chair, she broke your throne and she cut your hair,
And from your lips she drew the Hallelujah.

3. Baby, I've been here before, I've seen this room and I've walked this floor.
Y'know, I used to live alone before I knew ya.
And I've seen your flag on the marble arch, and love is not a victory march.
It's a cold and it's a broken Hallelujah.

4. Well, there was a time when you let me know what's really going on below,
But now you never show that to me, do you?
But remember when I moved in you, and the holy dove was moving too,
And every breath we drew was Hallelujah.

5. Maybe there's a God above, but all I've ever learned from love
Was how to shoot somebody who outdrew ya.
And it's not a cry that you hear at night, it's not somebody who's seen the light,
It's a cold and it's a broken Hallelujah.

House of the Rising Sun

Southern American Folksong

The Animals scored a pop hit with "House of the Rising Sun" in 1964, but it was first recorded in 1933 by North Carolina banjo/guitar picker, Clarence Ashley, and the song is much older than that. It was recorded in the 1930s, '40s and '50s by Roy Acuff, Woody Guthrie, Josh White, Leadbelly, The Weavers, Frankie Laine, as well as 1960s versions by Joan Baez and Bob Dylan (on his first album), and the list goes on. It's about a brothel, or a woman's prison, or something else! The arrangement below has a slow shuffle beat feel.

Additional Lyrics

2. My mother was a tailor, she sewed my old blue jeans.
   My father was a gambling man, down in New Orleans.

3. The only thing a gambler needs is a suitcase and a trunk,
   And the only time he's satisfied is when he's on a drunk.

4. Go and tell my baby sister not to do what I have done,
   And shun that house in New Orleans they call the Rising Sun.

5. I'm going back to New Orleans, my race is nearly run.
   I'm going to spend the rest of my life beneath the Rising Sun.

I Never Will Marry

Traditional Folksong

The Carter Family recorded this mournful ballad in 1933, but its roots may be in a two-hundred-year-old English tune, "The Lover's Lament for Her Sailor." A long list of folk, country and pop artists have covered it over the years, notably Joan Baez, Linda Ronstadt, Loretta Lynn and hundreds more! You can hear Mike Seeger play it on autoharp, accompanying his half-brother Pete Seeger on the *Hootenanny at Carnegie Hall* album.

Additional Lyrics

2. My love's gone and left me, he's the one I adore.
   He's gone where I never will see him anymore.
   Then she plunged her fair body in the ocean so deep.
   She closed her pretty blue eyes in the waters to keep.

I Will Always Love You

Words and Music by Dolly Parton

Dolly Parton scored a Number One hit with "I Will Always Love You" twice: once in 1974, when it was
first released, and again in 1982 when it was featured in the film *The Best Little Whorehouse in Texas*.
She wrote it the same day she wrote her signature song, "Jolene." When Whitney Houston sang it in the
1992 film *The Bodyguard*, the song went to #1 again, and became one of the biggest-selling singles of all time.

Slow rock ballad

1. If I should stay, I would on-ly be in your way, so I'll go, but I know I'll think of you each step of the way. And I will al-ways love you, I will al-ways love you.

2. Bit-ter -

3. you. I will al-ways love you.

Additional Lyrics

2. Bitter-sweet memories, that's all I'm taking with me.
Good-bye, please don't cry. We both know that I'm not what you need.

3. I hope life treats you kind, and I hope that you have all that you ever dreamed of.
And I wish you joy and happiness, but above all this, I wish you love.

I'll Fly Away

Words and Music by Albert E. Brumley

Possibly the most recorded gospel song of all time (and not just in the bluegrass world), "I'll Fly Away" goes back to the 1920s. Its inclusion in the 2000 film *O Brother, Where Art Thou?* gave it new life and inspired subsequent recordings by many more artists.

Verse

1. Some bright morning when this life is o'er,
2.–4. *See additional lyrics*

I'll fly away, to that home on God's celestial shore, I'll fly away.

Chorus

I'll fly away, oh, glory, I'll fly away in the morning. When I die, hallelujah bye and bye, I'll fly away.

Additional Lyrics

2. When the shadows of this life have grown, I'll fly away.
   Like a bird from prison walls has flown, I'll fly away.

3. Oh, how glad and happy when we meet. I'll fly away.
   No more cold iron shackles on my feet. I'll fly away.

4. Just a few more weary days and then I'll fly away.
   To land where joys will never end. I'll fly away.

I'm So Lonesome I Could Cry

Words and Music by Hank Williams

Hank Williams often called "I'm So Lonesome I Could Cry" his favorite record, and critics cite its lyrics to prove that country music can be beautiful poetry. Recorded in 1949, Williams wrote it as a poem for one of his "Luke the Drifter" recitations with musical background. Fortunately, he changed his mind, sang it to a beautiful melody, and made it one of country music's best-loved and most-recorded songs. It has been covered by such diverse artists as Al Green, Marty Robbins, Glen Campbell, Johnny Cash, the Cowboy Junkies, Leon Russell, B.J. Thomas and Jerry Lee Lewis.

Verse
Slow Waltz

1. Hear _____ that lone - some whip - poor - will, _____ he
   nev - er seen _____ a night _____ so long, _____ when
3., 4. See additional lyrics

sounds _____ too blue _____ to fly. The
time _____ goes crawl - ing by. The

mid - night train _____ is whin - ing low. I'm so
moon just went _____ be - hind the clouds to

1., 2., 3.   4.

lone - some I _____ could cry.   2. I've
hide his face _____ and cry.   3. Did you

Additional Lyrics

3. Did you ever see a robin weep when leaves begin to die?
   Like me, he's lost the will to live. I'm so lonesome I could cry.

4. The silence of a falling star lights up a purple sky,
   And as I wonder where you are, I'm so lonesome I could cry.

Keep on the Sunny Side

Words and Music by A.P. Carter

Written in 1899, this song was adapted and recorded by the Carter Family in 1928, and it eventually became their theme song. The song's composer, Ada Blenkhorn, got the title and idea for "Keep on the Sunny Side" from her disabled nephew, who always wanted his wheelchair pushed on the sunny side of the street. An image of a 78 rpm record is carved on the tombstone of Sara Carter, who traded autoharp duties with Maybelle on their many recordings, and on the record are the words "Keep on the Sunny Side." You can hear Maybelle solo on the song on Lester Flatt and Earl Scruggs' album *Songs of the Famous Carter Family*, on which Maybelle plays guitar and autoharp on many selections.

Verse

Brightly, in 2

1. There's a dark and a trou-bled side of life.
2., 3. *See additional lyrics*
There's a bright and a sun-ny side, too. Though we meet with the dark-ness and strife, ___ the sun-ny side we al-so may view.

Chorus

Keep on the sun-ny side, al-ways on the sun-ny side. Keep on the sun-ny side of life. It will help us ev-'ry day, it will bright-en all our way if we keep on the sun-ny side of life.

1., 2.

3.

2. Though a

Additional Lyrics

2. Though a storm and its fury break today, crushing hopes that we cherished so dear,
   Clouds and storm will in time pass away, the sun again will shine bright and clear.

3. Let us greet with a song of hope each day, though the moment be cloudy or fair.
   Let us trust in our Savior away, who keepeth everyone in His care.

Imagine

Words and Music by John Lennon

In 1971, John Lennon and Yoko Ono co-wrote "Imagine," the ultimate expression of idealism and faith in human nature. It was featured on the 1972 album of the same name, which was co-produced by John, Yoko and Phil Spector. The song became Lennon's biggest selling post-Beatles single, but more importantly, it has taken on anthemic status all over the world. The song has won quite a few awards and appears on countless "best songs of all time" lists, although the Edenic world it describes is highly controversial, if you think about it (no religion, no possessions, no countries). Lennon said that the lyrics and musical presentation "sugar coated" the radical message and made the song appealing to a worldwide audience. It has been performed and recorded by hundreds of famous artists.

Chorus

you may say _____ I'm a dream - er,

but I'm not the on - ly one. _____

I hope some day _____ you'll join us, _____ and the world _____ will

1.

2.

D.S.
(take 2nd ending)

be as one.

rit.

live as one. _____

Additional Lyrics

3. Imagine no possessions. I wonder if you can.
   No need for greed or hunger, a brotherhood of man.
   Imagine all the people sharing all the world.

Just When I Needed You Most

Words and Music by Randall VanWarmer

In 1979, singer/songwriter Randy VanWarmer scored a #1 hit with "Just When I Needed You Most," a song he co-wrote with Tony Wilson about a breakup with his girlfriend. He said that John Sebastian's autoharp instrumental break in the middle of the recording helped make the tune a hit. Dolly Parton must have agreed; when she covered the song in 1996, she had Sebastian reprise his autoharp solo. A long list of famous rock, country and R&B artists have recorded or performed the song.

Verse
Moderate Rock

1. You packed in the morn - ing and I stared out the win - dow and I
2., 3. *See additional lyrics*

strug - gled for some - thing to say. You left in the rain with - out

clos - ing the door. I did - n't stand in your way.

Now I miss you more than I

missed you be - fore, and now, where I'll find com - fort, God

knows. 'Cause you left me,

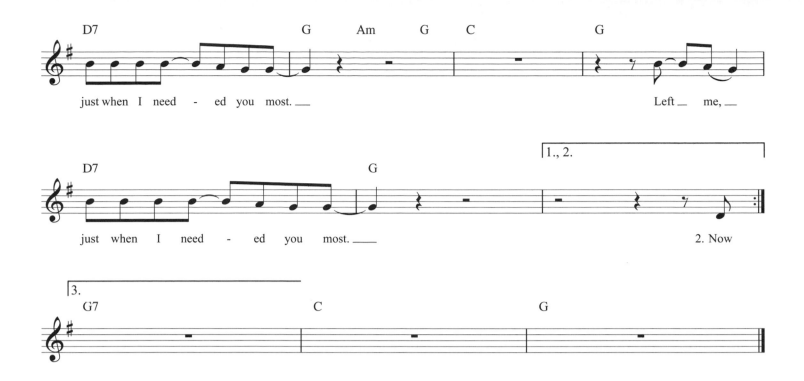

Additional Lyrics

2. Now most every morning I stare out the window and I think about where you might be.
   I've written you letters that I'd like to send, if you'd just send one to me.
   'Cause I need you more than I needed before and now, where I'll find comfort, God knows,
   'Cause you left me just when I needed you most.

3. You packed in the morning and I stared out the window and I struggled for something to say.
   You left in the rain without closing the door. I didn't stand in your way.
   Now I love you more than I loved you before and now, where I'll find comfort, God knows,
   'Cause you left me just when I needed you most.
   Oh, yeah, you left me just when I needed you most.

Let's Get Together
(Get Together)

Words and Music by Chet Powers

A genuine hippie anthem, "Get Together" had already been recorded by several mid-1960s folk and pop artists (The Kingston Trio, David Crosby, We Five, the Chad Mitchell Trio and Jefferson Airplane) before the Youngbloods' famous version was released in 1967 (a year known in the San Francisco Bay area as "The Summer of Love"). Re-released three years later, it rose to #5 on the pop charts. Renowned autoharpist (she's in the Autoharp Hall of Fame) Cathy Britell has recorded a beautiful arrangement of the tune.

Chorus

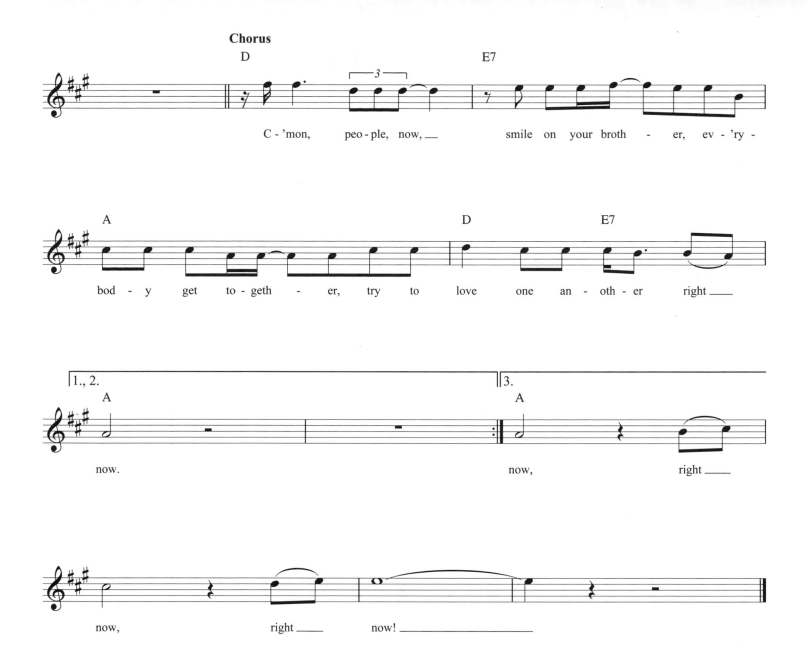

C - 'mon, peo - ple, now, ___ smile on your broth - er, ev - 'ry -

bod - y get to - geth - er, try to love one an - oth - er right ___

1., 2.
now.

3.
now, right ___

now, right ___ now! _____

Additional Lyrics

3. If you hear the song I sing, you will understand:
   You hold the key to love and fear, all in your tremblin' hand.
   Just one key unlocks them both; it's there at your command.

Love Me Tender

Words and Music by Elvis Presley and Vera Matson

In 1956, Academy Award-winning film score composer Ken Darby wrote a new set of lyrics for an old American ballad called "Aura Lea" (published in 1861). The result was the first pop single to sell a million copies *before* being released, Elvis Presley's "Love Me Tender." The song was featured in Presley's first film appearance, the 1956 *Love Me Tender*, which would eventually be followed by thirty more movies. Like many of the songs in this book, an interminable list of famous singers of many genres have recorded the ballad, and it has been featured in at least twenty films.

Additional Lyrics

2. Love me tender, love me long, take me to your heart.
   For it's there that I belong, and we'll never part.

3. Love me tender, love me, dear, tell me you are mine.
   I'll be yours through all the years, 'til the end of time.

Over the Rainbow

from THE WIZARD OF OZ

Music by Harold Arlen
Lyric by E.Y. "Yip" Harburg

Written by Harold Arlen and Yip Harburg for the 1939 classic film *The Wizard of Oz*, "Over the Rainbow" became Judy Garland's signature song because of her unforgettable, plaintive performance in the movie. As a team, and individually, Arlen and Harburg composed a long list of songs that have become standards in the "Great American Songbook." "Over the Rainbow" has enjoyed recent popularity because of Israel Kamakawiwo'ole's 1993 recording, which he played as a medley with "What a Wonderful World." Several autoharp virtuosi have recorded or performed the tune, including Adam Miller, Will Smith and Bill Bryant.

Make You Feel My Love

Words and Music by Bob Dylan

Bob Dylan included this love song on his 1997 *Time Out of Mind* album, and it is well on its way to becoming an American standard, having been recorded by over 450 artists to date. Billy Joel covered the tune before the release of *Time Out of Mind*, and Garth Brooks and Adele both scored major hits with the ballad.

§ **Bridge**

I know you have-n't made your mind up yet, ___
The storms are rag - ing on the roll - ing sea, ___

but I would nev - er do you wrong.
and on the high-way of re - gret.

I've known it from the mo - ment
The winds of change are blow - ing

that we met. ___
wild and free. ___

No doubt in my mind where you be - long.
You ain't seen noth - in' like me yet.

Verse

2. I'd go hun - gry, I'd go black and blue, ___
3. I could make you hap - py, make your dreams come true. ___

I'd go crawl-ing down the
No, there's noth - ing that I

av - e - nue.
would - n't do, ___

No, there's noth - ing I would - n't do, ___
go to the ends of the earth for you, ___

To Coda ⊕   *D.S. al Coda*   ⊕ **Coda**

to make you feel my love. ___

___

Man of Constant Sorrow

Traditional

"Man of Constant Sorrow" was published in a songbook in 1913, and was performed and recorded by many string bands and solo folk musicians in the ensuing decades. Bob Dylan included it in his first (1962) LP. The Stanley Brothers' 1959 recording was the template for the version in the 2000 film, *O Brother, Where Art Thou?*, which became a million-selling hit. You can see Mike Seeger perform the song on the autoharp, playing on his half-brother Pete's *Rainbow Quest* television program.

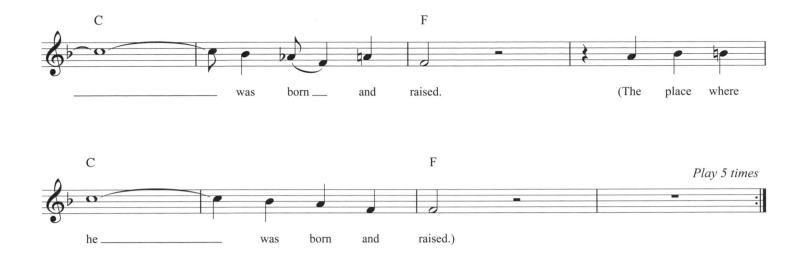

Additional Lyrics

2. For six long years I've been in trouble, no pleasure here on earth I find.
   For in this world I'm bound to ramble. I have no friends to help me now.
   (He has no friends to help him now.)

3. It's fare thee well, my own true lover. I never expect to see you again.
   For I'm bound to ride that northern railroad. Perhaps I'll die upon this train.
   (Perhaps he'll die upon this train.)

4. You can bury me in some deep valley, for many years where I may lay.
   Then you may learn to love another, while I am sleeping in my grave.
   (While he is sleeping in his grave.)

5. Maybe your friends think I'm just a stranger, my face you never will see no more.
   But there is one promise that is given: I'll meet you on God's golden shore.
   (He'll meet you on God's golden shore.)

Me and Bobby McGee

Words and Music by Kris Kristofferson and Fred Foster

Fred Foster, the president of Kris Kristofferson's record company (Monument Records) suggested the title, and Kristofferson came up with the song while driving in the rain. Roger Miller's 1969 recording of "Me and Bobby McGee" hit #12 on the country charts, and there were other covers by Gordon Lightfoot, Kenny Rogers and the Statler Brothers. Janis Joplin recorded the song in 1970, just before she died; her version was a huge posthumous hit. It made the song a major American ballad, and according to Kristofferson, it boosted his career significantly. He went on to write hundreds of songs including many hits for other artists, and he starred in many major Hollywood films.

Verse
Brightly, in 2

1. Bust-ed flat in Ba-ton Rouge, head-in' for the trains,
2. *See additional lyrics*

feel-in' near-ly fad-ed as my jeans.

Bob-by thumbed a die-sel down, just be-fore it rained,

took us all the way to New Or-leans.

I pulled my har-poon out of my dirt-y red ban-dan-na and was

blow-in' sad while Bob-by sang the blues. With them

Additional Lyrics

2. From the coal mines of Kentucky to the California sun,
   Bobby shared the secrets of my soul.
   Standin' right beside me, Lord, through everything I done,
   Every night she kept me from the cold.
   Then somewhere near Salinas, Lord, I let her slip away,
   Lookin' for the home I hope she'll find.
   And I'd trade all of my tomorrows for a single yesterday,
   Holdin' Bobby's body next to mine.

Me and the Wildwood Rose

Words and Music by Carlene Carter

Carlene Carter is the daughter of June Carter and June's first husband, country singer Carl Smith. She's released many chart-topping albums and singles, mostly self-penned. She wrote "Me and the Wildwood Rose" as a tribute to her grandmother, the legendary Maybelle Carter. Look for the YouTube video of Carlene Carter playing autoharp (like her grandmother used to) on a live performance of this tune.

Additional Lyrics

3. We'd be way down the road by the break of dawn,
   Biscuits and gravy and a truck stop song.
   In a world all my own I saw what I saw,
   And in the rearview mirror I'd get a wink from my Grandma.

4. Oh, I'll always remember the day that she died.
   My daddy, he called me and he started to cry.
   I rode on an airplane with all of my pain.
   My tears would not stop. We stood in a circle and sang.

Mr. Bojangles

Words and Music by Jerry Jeff Walker

Bill "Bojangles" Robinson, an African-American tap dancer, was very popular in the 1930s, appearing in many movies. His nickname became a generic term for black street dancers. One such dancer met Jerry Jeff Walker, a troubadour/songwriter, in jail in the 1960s, and inspired Walker to compose this song. The folk/rock Nitty Gritty Dirt Band had a Top Ten hit with "Mr. Bojangles" in 1970, and it became a staple of Sammy Davis Jr.'s performances. Countless artists have recorded it, including Whitney Houston, Elton John, Neil Diamond, Dolly Parton and William Shatner (!), despite the fact that, as Walker said, "It broke all the rules: it was too long, was in 6/8 time, about an old drunk and a dead dog."

Additional Lyrics

3. He said his name, Bojangles, and he danced a lick across the cell.
He grabbed his pants, a better stance, oh, he jumped so high, he clicked his heels.
He let go a laugh, he let go a laugh, shook back his clothes all around.

4. He danced for those at minstrel shows and county fairs throughout the South.
He spoke through tears of fifteen years, how his dog and him travelled about.
His dog up and died, he up and died. After twenty years, he still grieves.

5. He said, I dance now at every chance in honky-tonks, for drinks and tips.
But most the time I spend behind these county bars, 'cause I drinks a bit.
He shook his head, and as he shook his head, I heard someone ask, "Please...

Puff the Magic Dragon

Words and Music by Lenny Lipton and Peter Yarrow

"Puff, the Magic Dragon" was written by Peter Yarrow and a college roommate before the Peter, Paul and Mary group existed. The folk trio's recording of the song was a #2 pop hit in 1962, and it has been made into a TV special and a book. It remains a classic children's song, and both Peter and Paul Stookey have always denied that this story about loss of childish innocence has anything to do with marijuana, despite persistent, popular rumors.

Additional Lyrics

2. Together, they would travel on a boat with billowed sail.
   Jackie kept a lookout, perched on Puff's gigantic tail.
   Noble kings and princes would bow whene'er they came.
   Pirate ships would lower their flags when Puff roared out his name.

3. A dragon lives forever, but not so little boys.
   Painted wings and giant's rings make way for other toys.
   One gray night it happened, Jackie Paper came no more,
   And Puff, that mighty dragon, he ceased his fearless roar.

4. His head was bent in sorrow, green scales fell like rain.
   Puff no longer went to play along the cherry lane.
   Without his lifelong friend, Puff could not be brave.
   So Puff, that mighty dragon, sadly slipped into his cave.

Ripple

Words by Robert Hunter
Music by Jerry Garcia

With music by Jerry Garcia and lyrics by Robert Hunter (who wrote many songs for the Grateful Dead), "Ripple" first appeared on the classic 1970 *American Beauty* LP. One of the Dead's most beloved and popular songs, "Ripple" contains words and images from the 23rd Psalm and conveys a very friendly, spiritual/philosophical message, despite its existential slant (no mean feat!).

Additional Lyrics

2. Reach out your hand, if your cup be empty. If your cup is full, may it be again.
   Let it be known: there is a fountain that was not made by the hands of men.
   There is a road, no simple highway, between the dawn and the dark of night,
   and if you go, no one may follow. That path is for your steps alone.

3. You who choose to lead must follow, but if you fall, you fall alone.
   If you should stand, then who's to guide you? If I knew the way, I would take you home.
   La, dee, da, da, da, la, da, da, da, da, la, da, da, la, da, la, da, da, da, da.
   La, dee, da, da, da, la, da, da, da, da, la, da, da, la, da, da, da, da.

Scarborough Fair/Canticle

Arrangement and Original Counter Melody by Paul Simon and Arthur Garfunkel

Most people know "Scarborough Fair" from Simon and Garfunkel's 1966 version, which became a pop hit when it was used in the film, *The Graduate*. It's a traditional English ballad that goes back centuries, and it had already been well covered in films and folk and commercial recordings, notably by Peggy Seeger and Ewan McCall, before the Simon and Garfunkel version. Multi-instrumentalist/folksinger/autoharp contest winner Harvey Reid has a beautiful instrumental/autoharp version of the song on his album *The Autoharp Waltz*.

Verse
Moderate Waltz

1. Are you go - ing to Scar - bor - ough Fair?
2., 3., 4. *See additional lyrics*

Pars - ley, sage, rose - mar - y and thyme. Re -

mem - ber me to one who lives there. ___

She once was a true love of mine.

Play 4 times

Additional Lyrics

2. Tell her to make me a cambric shirt. Parsley, sage, rosemary and thyme.
   Without no seams nor needlework. Then she'll be a true love of mine.

3. Tell her to find me an acre of land. Parsley, sage, rosemary and thyme.
   Between the salt water and the sea strands. Then she'll be a true love of mine.

4. Tell her to reap it with a sickle of leather. Parsley, sage, rosemary and thyme.
   And gather it all in a bunch of heather. Then she'll be a true love of mine.

Simple Gifts

Traditional Shaker Hymn

The Shakers are a Christian sect, founded in England in 1747, who were ahead of their time with their communal, pacifist and egalitarian (equal rights for women!) beliefs and lifestyle. Two American Shakers wrote "Simple Gifts" in 1848, and it remains an often-covered folk classic. Aaron Copland used the melody in the 1944 Ballet, *Appalachian Spring*, and many folk, rock and pop artists have recorded it or used fragments of it in their original songs. That would include Judy Collins, Weezer, R.E.M., The Turtles, Jewel, Yo-Yo Ma and Alison Krauss, and many more. You can find beautiful autoharp versions of "Simple Gifts" on YouTube, performed by Autoharp Hall of Famers Will Smith (not the actor!) and Bryan Bowers (plus many other excellent players).

Stand by Me

Words and Music by Jerry Leiber, Mike Stoller and Ben E. King

In 1960, having just left his R&B group, the Drifters, singer Ben E. King brought a fragment of an old gospel song to the very successful songwriting team Leiber and Stoller. The three of them came up with "Stand by Me," which was an immediate, international hit. Revived in 1986 by its inclusion in the movie *Stand by Me*, it was a Top Ten hit for a new generation, and it has become one of the most-performed pop songs of the 20th century. Besides being recorded by hundreds of artists (including a stellar turn by John Lennon), it is often performed at weddings…including Prince Harry and Meghan Markle's 2018 marriage at Windsor Castle.

Additional Lyrics

2. If the sky that we look upon should tumble and fall,
   Or the mountain should crumble to the sea,
   I won't cry, I won't cry, no, I won't shed a tear,
   Just as long as you stand by me.

Tennessee Waltz

Words and Music by Redd Stewart and Pee Wee King

Pee Wee King and Redd Stewart were inspired by Bill Monroe's "Kentucky Waltz" when they wrote and recorded "Tennessee Waltz" in 1947, and in the next few years it was a Top Ten hit on the country charts for the composer/performers, and for Cowboy Copas and Roy Acuff. Patti Page had a pop hit with the tune in 1951, and it is often credited with bringing a larger urban audience to country music. Many artists have had hits recording "Tennessee Waltz," and in 1965 it became Tennessee's official state song. Maybelle Carter plays an instrumental autoharp version, unaccompanied on her *Wildwood Pickin'* album.

Suzanne

Words and Music by Leonard Cohen

"Suzanne" is one of Canadian poet/singer-songwriter Leonard Cohen's most popular tunes. Judy Collins'
1965 recording of the song was a folk hit, and it made the public aware of Cohen's songwriting talent. It
has been covered by singers as diverse as Harry Belafonte, Neil Diamond, Tori Amos and Peter Gabriel.

Verse
Moderately slow rock

1. Su - zanne takes you down ____ to her place by the riv - er. You can
2., 3. *See additional lyrics*

hear the boats go by, ___ you can spend the night for - ev - er, and you

know that she's half cra - zy, ___ and that's why you want to be there, and she

feeds you tea and or - ang - es that come all the way from Chi - na. And

just when you want to tell her that you have no love to give her, she

Additional Lyrics

2. And Jesus was a sailor when he walked upon the water,
And he spent a long time watching from his lonely wooden tower,
And when he knew for certain only drowning men could see him,
He said "All men will be sailors then until the sea shall free them."
But he himself was broken, long before the sky would open.
Forsaken, almost human, he sank beneath your wisdom like a stone.
And you want to travel with him, and you want to travel blind,
And you think maybe you'll trust him,
For he's touched your perfect body with his mind.

3. Now, Suzanne takes your hand and she leads you to the river.
She's wearing rags and feathers from Salvation Army counters.
And the sun pours down like honey on Our Lady of the Harbor,
And she shows you where to look among the garbage and the flowers.
There are heroes in the seaweed, there are children in the morning.
They are leaning out for love and they will lean that way forever,
While Suzanne holds her mirror.
And you want to travel with her, and you want to travel blind,
And you know that you can trust her,
For she's touched your perfect body with her mind.

Sweet Caroline

Words and Music by Neil Diamond

Neil Diamond wrote "Sweet Caroline" in an hour in a Memphis hotel room, because he only had two songs prepared for the next day's recording session, and a third song was required. It's one of a long list of Neil Diamond hits, and is ritually sung at Fenway Park's Red Sox games. It has been recorded by Waylon Jennings, The Drifters, Julio Iglesias, Elvis Presley and many more stars, but Diamond's favorite version is Frank Sinatra's big band rendition.

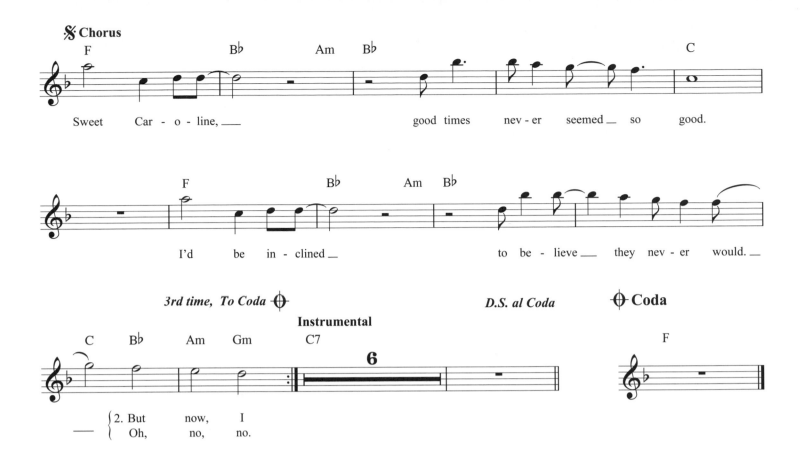

Sweet Car - o - line, ___ good times nev - er seemed ___ so good.

I'd be in - clined ___ to be - lieve ___ they nev - er would. ___

3rd time, To Coda ⊕   *D.S. al Coda*   ⊕ **Coda**

Instrumental

C   Bb   Am   Gm   C7   **6**   F

___ 2. But now, I

Oh, no, no.

Take Me Home, Country Roads

Words and Music by John Denver, Bill Danoff and Taffy Nivert

Even though he'd never been to West Virginia, in 1970 a relatively unknown John Denver helped his
friends Bill and Taffy Danoff finish their song, "Take Me Home, Country Roads" (they'd never been
there either!). They recorded the tune in New York, and the following year it moved slowly up the charts,
ultimately becoming a huge hit and Denver's signature song…and one of West Virginia's official state songs.

Teach Your Children

Words and Music by Graham Nash

From the 1970 Crosby, Stills, Nash and Young album, *Déjà Vu*, this very popular tune featured Jerry Garcia on pedal steel. Graham Nash wrote it when he was in The Hollies, during the Vietnam war, while reflecting on violence in the world, and the importance of parental guidance.

Additional Lyrics

2. And you of tender years can't know the fears that your elders grew by.
And so please help them with your youth. They seek the truth before they can die.
Teach your parents well. Their children's hell will slowly go by,
And feed them on your dreams. The one they pick's the one you'll know by.
Don't you ever ask them why. If they told you, you would cry,
So just look at them and sigh, and know they love you.

This Land Is Your Land

Words and Music by Woody Guthrie

The first part of the melody of Woody Guthrie's anthemic song resembles a Carter Family tune called "Little Darlin' Pal of Mine." Woody wrote the song in 1940 and recorded it a few years later. It was recorded by most of the well-known 1960s folksingers. In later years, it has been covered by rockers, funk/soul bands, country musicians, and has become one of the most famous folk songs of all time, often taught in public schools all over the U.S.

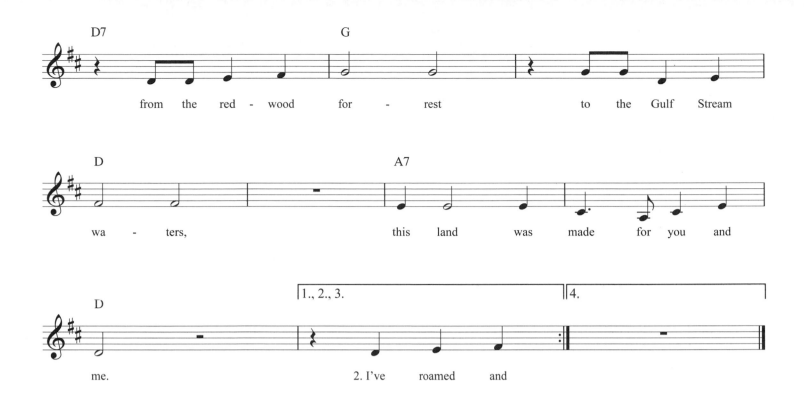

from the red - wood for - rest to the Gulf Stream
wa - ters, this land was made for you and
me. 2. I've roamed and

Additional Lyrics

2. I've roamed and rambled, and I've followed my footsteps
   To the sparkling sands of her diamond deserts.
   And all around me, a voice was sounding:
   This land was made for you and me.

3. The sun comes shining, as I was strolling,
   The wheat fields waving and the dust clouds rolling.
   The fog was lifting, a voice come chanting:
   This land was made for you and me.

4. As I was walkin', I saw a sign there,
   And that sign said "No trespassin',"
   But on the other side, it didn't say nothin'!
   Now that side was made for you and me!

Chorus 4. In the squares of the city, in the shadow of the steeple,
   Near the relief office, I see my people.
   And some are grumblin' and some are wonderin'
   If this land's still made for you and me.

Tumbling Tumbleweeds

Words and Music by Bob Nolan

Though many people know "Tumbling Tumbleweeds" because it begins and ends the movie
The Big Lebowski, it was made famous in the early 1930s by the singing cowboy group, The Sons of
the Pioneers. It became their theme song, and one of the most famous cowboy songs, but it has even
been recorded by jazz artists like Harry James and Grant Green, pop stars like Frankie Laine, Bing
Crosby, The Supremes, actor Clint Eastwood and punk rockers The Meat Puppets… among many others.

Wayfaring Stranger

Southern American Folk Hymn

This gospel favorite goes back to the early 1800s, possibly earlier. It was sung at Appalachian revival services and spread west with the pioneers. Later, folksinger Burl Ives popularized it in the 1940s, followed by Joan Baez in the '60s, Emmylou Harris in the '80s, and Johnny Cash in 2000...and more recently, Ed Sheeran's cover has been widely viewed on YouTube. Bill Monroe recorded and performed many versions of it from the 1950s until his last years. Harvey Reid, Bill Bryant and many other autoharpists have performed the song.

Additional Lyrics

2. I know dark clouds will gather 'round me; I know my way is rough and steep.
   But beautiful fields lie just beyond me, where souls redeemed their vigil keep.
   I'm going there to meet my mother, she said she'd meet me when I come.
   I'm just a-going over Jordan, I'm only going over home.

Turn! Turn! Turn!
(To Everything There Is a Season)

Words from the Book of Ecclesiastes
New Words by Toshi Seeger
Adaptation and Music by Pete Seeger

Pete Seeger wrote the tune in 1959, adapting prose from the Bible's *Book of Ecclesiastes*. It was first recorded in 1962 by the folk trio, The Limeliters, and in 1965, The Byrds electrified it and made it a #1 pop hit. It also charted in Europe, and it has been covered by many artists.

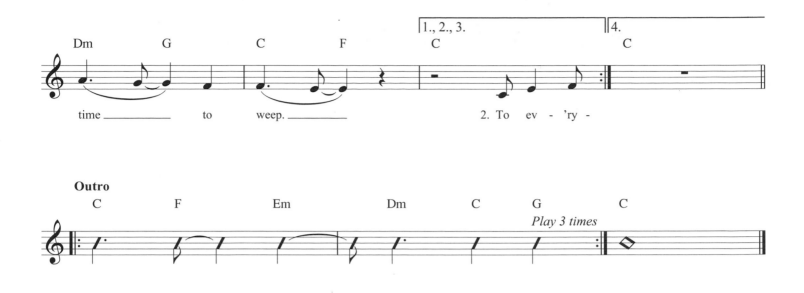

Additional Lyrics

2. To everything, turn, turn, turn, there is a season, turn, turn, turn.
   And a time for every purpose under heaven.
   A time to build up, a time to break down, a time to dance, a time to mourn.
   A time to cast away stones, a time to gather stones together.

3. To everything, turn, turn, turn, there is a season, turn, turn, turn.
   And a time to every purpose under heaven.
   A time of love, a time of hate, a time of war, a time of peace.
   A time you may embrace, a time to refrain from embracing.

4. To everything, turn, turn, turn, there is a season, turn, turn, turn.
   And a time for every purpose under heaven.
   A time to gain, a time to lose, a time to rend, a time to sew.
   A time of love, a time of hate, a time for peace, I swear it's not too late.

What a Wonderful World

Words and Music by George David Weiss and Bob Thiele

This song has had many lives: Louis Armstrong's wonderful 1968 recording of "What a Wonderful World" reached #1 on the U.K. charts, but had little success in the U.S. until it was used in the 1987 film *Good Morning Vietnam*. Joey Ramone recorded a hard rock/punk version in 2002 and performed it often in concert. Singer/guitarist Eva Cassidy had a posthumous hit with the song in 2007, and in 1993, Hawaiian musician Israel Kamakawiwoʻole did his own interpretation as part of a medley with *Over the Rainbow*. Used in several movies, television shows and commercials, Iz's medley became a huge hit. It was a significant factor in the ukulele renaissance that is still going strong, despite the fact that he recorded it at three in the morning in one take with just his voice and ukulele…no big production, no samples! World-renowned autoharpist Ray Choi has a performance of "What a Wonderful World" on YouTube that is inspired by Armstrong's version.

When I Go

Words and Music by Dave Carter

Written by highly-acclaimed American singer/songwriter Dave Carter, who performed often with
Tracy Grammer, "When I Go" appeared on Carter's 1998 album of the same name. It has been recorded
by Judy Collins featuring Willie Nelson, and autoharp hero Bryan Bowers, one of the first inductees
into the Autoharp Hall of Fame. Bowers has helped popularize the autoharp since the 1980s. He brings
a suitcase full of autoharps to a performance and dazzles with his virtuoso stylings.

Verse
Moderately, in 2

1. Come, lone - ly hunt - er, chief - tan and king, I will
2., 3. *See additional lyrics*

fly like a fal - con, when I go. ____

Bear me, my broth - er, un - der your wing. I will

strike, fell like light - ning when I ____ go. 1. I will ____

Chorus

bel - low like the thun - der drum, in - voke the storm ____ of war, ____ a twist - in'
2.–4. *See additional lyrics*

Additional Lyrics

Verse 2. Spring, spirit dancer, nimble and thin, I will leap like coyote when I go.
Tireless entrancer, lend me your skin, I will run like the gray wolf when I go.

Chorus 2. I will climb the rise at daybreak, I will kiss the sky at noon,
Raise my yearning voice at midnight to my mother in the moon.
I will make the lay of long defeat and draw the chorus slow.
I'll send this message down the wire and hope that someone wise is listenin' when I go.

Chorus 3. And when the sun comes trumpets from his red house in the east,
He will find a standin' stone where long I chanted my release.
He will send his morning messenger to strike the hammer blow,
And I will crumble down uncountable in showers of crimson rubies when I go.

Verse 3. Sigh, mournful sister, whisper and turn, I will rattle like dry leaves when I go.
Stand in the mist where my fire used to burn, I will camp on the night breeze when I go.

Chorus 4. And should you glimpse my wandering form out on the borderline,
Between death and resurrection and the council of the pines,
Do not worry for my comfort, do not sorrow for me so.
All your diamond tears will rise up and adorn the sky beside me when I go.

Wildwood Flower

Words and Music by A.P. Carter

One of the Carter Family's most often-covered songs, "Wildwood Flower" was inspired by one or possibly two nineteenth-century parlor songs.* It became Maybelle Carter's signature tune, and for decades it was considered a rite of passage for an acoustic guitarist to learn how to pick the tune as an instrumental. Maybelle can be seen and/or heard on several of her albums or YouTube videos, playing the song on autoharp.

(Incidentally, the lyrics in the first verse often appear in books or online as "the pale amaryllis and islips so blue," or "the pale amanita..." or variations that sound botanical, but in multiple recordings, Maybelle and June Carter clearly sing "the pale and the leader and eyes look like blue"...whether or not it makes sense!)

*Songs sung around the piano for entertainment in the living room (parlor).

Additional Lyrics

2. I will dance, I will sing and my laugh shall be gay.
   I will charm ev'ry heart, in his crown I will sway.
   When I woke from the dreaming, my idol was clay.
   All portion of love had all flown away.

3. Oh, he taught me to love him and promised to love,
   And to cherish me over all others above.
   How my heart is now wondering, no misery can tell.
   He's left me no warning, no words of farewell.

4. Oh, he taught me to love him and called me his flower,
   That's blooming to cheer him through life's dreary hour.
   Oh, I long to see him and regret the dark hour.
   He's gone and neglected this pale wildwood flower.

Can the Circle Be Unbroken
(Will the Circle Be Unbroken)
Words and Music by A.P. Carter

In 1935, the Carter Family recorded "Can the Circle Be Unbroken," a revised version of a 1907 hymn ("Will the Circle Be Unbroken") in which the singer describes his or her mother's funeral and declares that we'll all be reunited in heaven. The Carter family arrangement has become extremely popular and is often sung as a finale to a country music or bluegrass concert. Numerous singers and bands of all genres have recorded the tune.

The verse and chorus share the same melody.

Additional Lyrics

2. Lord, I told the undertaker, "Undertaker, please drive slow,
   For this body you are hauling, Lord, I hate to see her go."

3. I followed close behind her, tried to hold up and be brave.
   But I could not hide my sorrow when they laid her in the grave.

4. Went back home, Lord, my home was lonesome, since my mother she was gone.
   All my brothers, sisters cryin', what a home so sad and lone.

The Wind and the Rain

Traditional English

Perhaps of Scottish origin, this old ballad has been performed and recorded with many lyric variations, but all versions tell the same grim story. Sometimes it's called "Oh the Wind and the Rain," or "The Two Sisters." There's an excellent autoharp version by Mike Seeger and other fine recordings by Peggy Seeger, Ethel Raim, Jody Stecher, Gillian Welch, Jerry Garcia and autoharp virtuoso Kilby Snow, among others. Snow recorded one album for Folkways Records in the 1960s that demonstrated his unique autoharp style and established him as an early autoharp icon, and one of the first inductees into the Autoharp Hall of Fame.

Verse

Brightly, in 2

1. 'Twas ear - ly one morn - ing in the month of May, oh, the wind and
3., 5., 7., 9. *See additional lyrics*

rain, two sis - ters went fish - in' on a hot sum - mer's day.

Oh, the dread - ful wind and rain.

Verse

2. These two sis - ters came a - walk - in' down the stream, oh, the wind and
4., 6., 8., 10. *See additional lyrics*

rain, and one came be - hind, pushed the oth - er one in, cry - in',

"Oh,   the   dread - ful   wind   and   rain."

Additional Lyrics

3. Johnny gave the youngest one a gold ring, oh, the wind and rain,
   But he didn't give the other one anything. Oh, the dreadful wind and rain.

4. Pushed her in the river to drown, oh, the wind and rain,
   And watched her as she floated down, cryin', "The dreadful wind and rain."

5. She floated on down to the miller's pond, oh, the wind and rain,
   Cryin', "Father, father, there swims a swan." Oh, the dreadful wind and rain.

6. The miller fished her out with his fishin' hook, oh, the wind and rain,
   And brought this maiden from the brook, cryin', "The dreadful wind and rain."

7. He laid her on the bank to dry, oh, the wind and rain,
   And a fiddler he came passing by, cryin', "The dreadful wind and rain."

8. The fiddler spied this maiden fair, oh, the wind and rain.
   He took thirty strands of her long yellow hair, cryin', "The dreadful wind and rain."

9. He made a fiddle of her little breast bone, oh, the wind and rain,
   With a sound that would melt a heart of stone, cryin', "The dreadful wind and rain."

10. And the only tune that fiddle would play, oh, the wind and rain,
    The only tune that fiddle would play was "Oh, the dreadful wind and rain."

Yesterday

Words and Music by John Lennon and Paul McCartney

On June 14, 1965, with his steel-stringed acoustic Epiphone guitar tuned down a whole step, Paul McCartney sang and played two takes of "Yesterday." The other three Beatles were not present, and George Martin talked Paul into adding a string quartet accompaniment to the second take. The result is probably the most-recorded popular song ever, with over 2,500 cover versions by every singer from Frank Sinatra to Daffy Duck. The melody came to Paul in a dream, and he wasn't sure whether he remembered it or wrote it, so he spent a month playing it for friends in the music business and asking if they had ever heard it before. While working on lyrics to a song, the Beatles often had a "dummy lyric" to get things rolling (which they knew they'd eventually replace), and Paul originally called this one "Scrambled Eggs," because his working lyric was "Scrambled eggs, oh my baby how I love your legs." A very unusual feature of "Yesterday": though it's written in the popular AABA form* the A phrase is only seven bars long. (Look for instrumental autoharp versions on YouTube by Will Smith and Ray Choi.)

*The AABA format usually consists of an eight bar-phrase (A), which is repeated with different lyrics, then a bridge (B—that the Beatles called the "middle eight"), and finally a repeat of the A part with different lyrics. This 32-bar format takes you once around the tune.

You Are My Sunshine

Words and Music by Jimmie Davis

One of the United States' most popular songs, "You Are My Sunshine" was made famous by country singer/governor of Louisiana, Jimmie Davis' 1940 recording. It has been covered by singers of all genres, including Bing Crosby, Ray Charles, Chuck Berry, The Beach Boys, Nat "King" Cole, Burl Ives, Gene Autry, Mississippi John Hurt, Mose Allison and many more! Listen to the first (1939) recording by the Pine Ridge Boys on YouTube, and the excellent instrumental version by autoharpist Ziggy Harpdust! This arrangement is in E♭, because that key allows you to play the optional, momentary D chord in the third bar.

Additional Lyrics

2. You told me once, dear, that you love me, that nothing else could come between.
   But now you've left me for another, and you've shattered all my dreams.

3. I'll always love you and make you happy, if you will only say the same.
   But if you leave me for another, you'll regret it all some day.

Your Cheatin' Heart

Words and Music by Hank Williams

Hank Williams' last recording session, in 1952, was attended by his fiancée, Billie Jean Jones, and his former girlfriend, Bobbie Jett, with an ex-boyfriend in tow. Bobbie Jett came uninvited to confront Hank—she was pregnant with his child. In this soap opera atmosphere, Williams recorded four songs, including "Your Cheatin' Heart." Probably written to his ex-wife Audrey, it became Hank's theme song after his death. He may have never performed this tune live, but it went to #1 on the charts, and many vocalists have charted with it over the years.